TECHNOLOGY TAKES ON NATURE

ICE ROADS

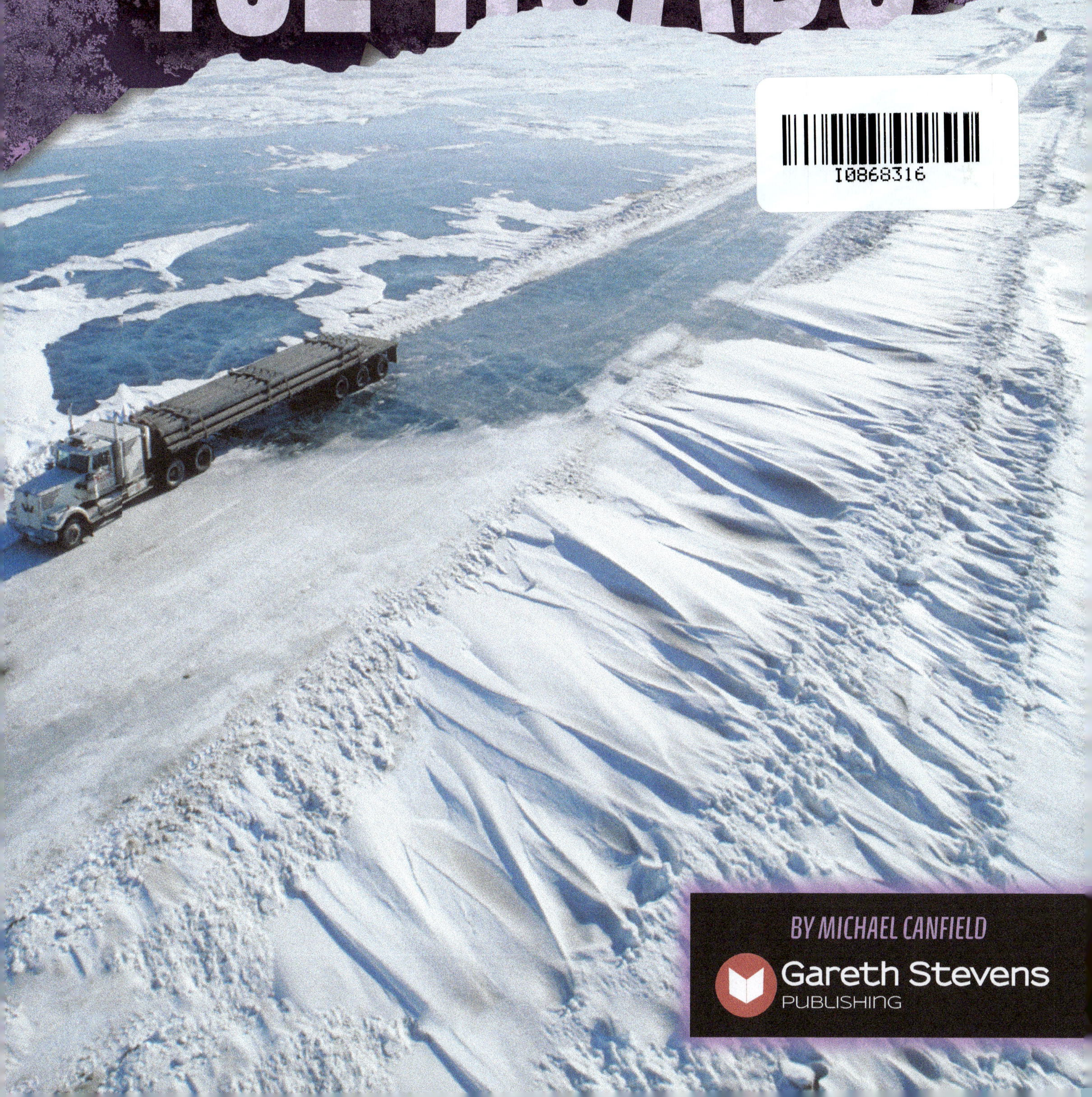

BY MICHAEL CANFIELD

Gareth Stevens PUBLISHING

Please visit our website, www.garethstevens.com. For a free color catalog of all our high-quality books, call toll free 1-800-542-2595 or fax 1-877-542-2596.

Cataloging-in-Publication Data

Names: Canfield, Michael.
Title: Ice roads / Michael Canfield.
Description: New York : Gareth Stevens Publishing, 2017. | Series: Technology takes on nature | Includes index.
Identifiers: ISBN 9781482457711 (pbk.) | ISBN 9781482457735 (library bound) | ISBN 9781482457728 (6 pack)
Subjects: LCSH: Truck drivers–Juvenile literature. | Trucking–Juvenile literature. | Trucking–Arctic regions–Juvenile literature. | Ice crossings–Juvenile literature.
Classification: LCC HD8039.M795 C325 2017 | DDC 388.3'4409113–dc23

First Edition

Published in 2017 by
Gareth Stevens Publishing
111 East 14th Street, Suite 349
New York, NY 10003

Designer: Sarah Liddell
Editor: Ryan Nagelhout

Photo credits: Cover, p. 1 Richard Olsenius/Getty Images; background texture used throughout Olga Miltsova/Shutterstock.com; p. 5 CambridgeBayWeather/Wikimedia Commons; p. 6 Popova Valeriya/Shutterstock.com; p. 7 Magnus Manske/Wikimedia Commons; p. 8 RAIGO PAJULA/Stringer/AFP/Getty Images; pp. 9, 13, 17, 27 James Reeves/Getty Images; p. 10 Pi-Lens/Shutterstock.com; p. 11 Richard Olsenius/Contributor/National Geographic/Getty Images; p. 12 pgaborphotos/Shutterstock.com; p. 14 Json Pineau/Getty Images; p. 15 mHanafiAhmad/Shutterstock.com; pp. 16, 21 Geo Swan/Wikimedia Commons; p. 18 MJ Preston/Wikimedia Commons; p. 19 Image by Nonac_Digi for the Green Man/Getty Images; p. 20 Eric CHRETIEN/Contributor/Gamma-Rapho/Getty Images; p. 22 Philippe Michel/Getty Images; p. 23 Johnny Haglund/Getty Images; p. 24 Sharingknowledge/Wikimedia Commons; p. 25 Aerohod/Wikimedia Commons; p. 29 boreala/Shutterstock.com.

Printed in the United States of America

CPSIA compliance information: Batch #CW17GS: For further information contact Gareth Stevens, New York, New York at 1-800-542-2595.

CONTENTS

Words in the glossary appear in **bold** type the first time they are used in the text.

ICY CONDITIONS

Mining is a large part of the economy in northern Canada. Many mines are separated from the mainland by large bodies of water. In summer, boats called ferries carry supplies and **equipment** to the mines and workers. In winter, however, the ferries are unable to travel over the frozen waters.

Some people have found a cool, but dangerous, answer to the problem—ice roads. Some of the first ice roads were made in northern Canada in the 1930s, and they're now used in cold areas of the United States, China, Russia, and many other countries. An ice road is exactly what it sounds like: a road of ice crossing frozen lakes and rivers!

KEEP ON TRUCKING

Today's ice roads are commonly used by large tractor-trailers and tanker trucks carrying fuel, supplies, and equipment to far-off mining communities. In the 1930s, however, tractors traveled as "trains," pulling sleds that carried heavy mining equipment. One of the first "trains" delivered 28 tons (25 mt) of mining equipment over the ice road.

THIS ICE ROAD ON THE GREAT SLAVE LAKE IN NORTHWESTERN CANADA RUNS BETWEEN THE TOWN OF YELLOWKNIFE AND A SMALL FISHING COMMUNITY.

ICE-ROAD BUILDERS

What goes into building an ice road? It's more than just making big ice cubes! For starters, the temperature needs to be right. It needs to be cold. Water freezes at 32°F (0°C), so any air temperature at or below that will form ice. When the ice atop a lake or river is about 1 foot (0.3 m) thick, ice-road builders can get to work.

Snowplows move any **insulating** snow off the ice, usually by late December. Taking the snow off the ice lets more ice form under it more quickly. As it grows colder, the ice becomes thicker. Soon, trucks can start driving on it.

KALLAVESI LAKE IN FINLAND DURING SUMMER

ICE-ROAD **EXPERTS** STUDY THE ROAD THROUGHOUT THE WINTER, CONTINUALLY MAKING SURE EVERYTHING IS SAFE.

ICE ROAD OVER KALLAVESI LAKE

ICE-ROAD EXPERTS

Ice roads can be dangerous, and it's up to the experts to decide when they're safe to drive on. It's an important job, as the wrong decision could send a truck driver through the ice! Experts measure the thickness of the ice, as well as **monitor** weather reports to see if the road needs more work done to keep drivers safe.

Throughout the process, ice-road builders and ice-road experts work 20-hour days, often in temperatures well below freezing. These engineers work to make sure the ice can handle the thousands of pounds of trucks and equipment traveling on it.

Most times, the roadway is made entirely out of ice over a body of water. When parts of an ice road don't get thick enough, however, engineers step in to help nature out. Sometimes ice and snow are packed down over a bed of gravel.

RIG MATS

One way engineers make ice roads stronger is by making a "rig mat." The mat is built by arranging steel and wooden beams in a **lattice** pattern. Then water is used to freeze it in place over a weak spot in the ice. This is often used in the middle of a lake where the ice isn't thick enough to support a truck.

NOT ALL ICE ROADS ARE MADE OF JUST ICE. RIG MATS, GRAVEL, AND OTHER MATERIALS CAN BE USED TO MAKE WEAK AREAS STRONG ENOUGH TO HOLD CARS AND TRUCKS.

SOME ICE ROADS, LIKE THIS ONE IN NORTHWESTERN CANADA, ARE ACTUALLY FLOODED WITH WATER BY WORKERS SO ANOTHER LAYER OF ICE CAN FREEZE QUICKLY TO STRENGTHEN THE SURFACE.

THE ICE BOWL

Ice roads need to be strong enough to keep trucks from breaking through, but also **flexible** enough to bend. As a heavy truck moves over ice, it pushes down on the ice and creates a depression, or bowl-shaped dip, in the ice. The faster a truck is moving, the bigger and deeper the depression.

Depending on temperature and ice thickness, at a certain point, that depression can cause waves of water under the ice that may damage the ice road above it. The first truck may make it across safely, but the next one driving across the road could fall in!

PRESSURE RIDGE

ICE-ROAD ENGINEERS OFTEN BUILD ROADS AT AN ANGLE TO NEARBY SHORELINES. THIS PREVENTS **BLOWOUTS** UNDER THE ROADBED, WHICH COULD CAUSE ACCIDENTS.

PRESSURE RIDGES

Pressure ridges happen when ice gets bigger (expands) or smaller (contracts) based on temperature changes. When ice gets warmer, the ice pushes out and may break, pushing up the ice and creating ridges. These pressure ridges weaken ice and may cause problems for ice roads.

WATCHING THE ICE

Once an ice road is built, it's monitored closely. Each day, a crew drives along the road to test its strength and thickness. A tool that bounces radio waves into the lake is dragged along the ice. A computer establishes how thick the ice is by measuring how long it takes for the signal to return.

Workers also drill holes, called boreholes, into the ice to see how thick it is. Scientists and engineers working on ice roads study how water moves and how temperature changes affect the roads. No one wants an ice road to fail!

BOREHOLE BEING DRILLED INTO ICE

DRIVING ON AN ICE SHEET AT THE RIGHT SPEED AND WITH THE RIGHT WEIGHT CAN ACTUALLY MAKE AN ICE ROAD STRONGER! DRIVERS CALL THIS "DRIVING DOWN THE FROST."

NO SEATBELTS

You should always wear a seatbelt in a car, but ice road truckers often don't because it could kill them! If a truck breaks through the ice, drivers only have a few seconds to get out before they drown or their body is shocked by freezing waters.

PRIZED LOADS

Ice roads are most important for companies working in areas that can only be reached by ice roads during winter. Supplies are needed to keep workers fed, clothed, and clean. Equipment is needed to keep the mine or other business going. Fuel is also needed to keep everything running.

Without the ice roads, businesses would have to shut down once ferries couldn't run in the frozen waters. Thanks to ice roads, new industries like diamond mining have sprung to life in Canada, which is now the third-largest producer of diamonds in the world!

EKATI DIAMOND MINE IN CANADA

FLYING IN HEAVY SUPPLIES IN BAD WEATHER WOULD BE MORE DANGEROUS THAN DRIVING ACROSS AN ICE ROAD. PLANES HAVE A MUCH HARDER TIME FIGHTING WIND AND SNOW THAN TRUCKS DO.

WHY NOT FLY?

While flying in supplies and equipment might seem like a better option than driving on ice roads, there are a few reasons why planes aren't used. The heavy weight of the supplies would cost a lot of money and be dangerous for pilots. It's also much more dangerous to fly in snowstorms than to drive!

STAYING SAFE

Keeping drivers safe is the most important part of building and maintaining an ice road. If the ice isn't thick enough, or if it starts to melt, trucks can fall through the ice. Driving on ice roads is dangerous, and people do die on the job.

Safety **precautions** are taken on ice roads to prevent accidents. Most ice roads have speed limits like regular roads, but they're much slower: 16 miles (26 km) per hour. This speed limit prevents the trucks from creating waves under the ice, which can make the ice crack.

ALONG WITH SPEED LIMITS, MANY ICE ROADS HAVE WEIGHT LIMITS. THIS ROAD IN NORTHWESTERN CANADA HAS A WEIGHT LIMIT OF ABOUT ABOUT 70 TONS (64 MT).

WHEN ICE ROADS AREN'T SAFE, TRUCKS CAN, AND DO, PLUNGE THROUGH THE ICE.

SLOW DOWN!

You might think going fast over ice gets the drive finished faster, but going the speed limit is important. Some ice roads—like one built on Waite Lake in Canada—only let drivers go a few miles per hour. Drivers must know these limits and keep to them to keep themselves and other drivers safe.

DRIVING ON ICE

Despite the danger, many truckers sign up to drive on ice from January to April each year. Why? They do it because even first-time drivers can make between $30,000 and $40,000 in a few months, and long-time drivers can bring home up to $80,000. That's a lot of money for just a few months' work!

The money, however, comes at a cost. Long drives between places make for sleepless days and tired nights. Fighting to stay awake is often part of the job, which makes it even more dangerous to drive on thick ice.

SLEEP?

Drivers on ice roads are required to take sleep breaks between 15-hour driving shifts. Usually, the driver is in between stops and has to sleep on a bed in their truck, called a bunk. Eight hours between shifts is the Canadian standard, although drivers often can split up their sleep time.

LOCKHART LAKE TRUCK STOP

MOST ICE-ROAD DRIVING IS DONE WHILE IT'S DARK BECAUSE COLD PLACES ARE OFTEN POINTING AWAY FROM THE SUN DURING WINTER DUE TO THE MOVEMENT OF EARTH. PLACES NEAR THE NORTH POLE MIGHT GET LITTLE OR NO SUNLIGHT EACH DAY!

WANNA HIT THE ROAD?

If you think the money is worth the risks, here are some tips on making it through a season on the ice roads. First, bring earplugs, because you'll hear the ice cracking underneath as you drive over it! And be prepared to be stuck out on the ice. Drivers are often caught up in severe winter storms called blizzards that make driving very unsafe. They could strike at any time!

Drivers will also see markers along some ice roads where other ice road truckers died due to accidents. What do you think? Can you hack it as an ice-road truck driver?

MANY ICE ROADS HAVE CROSSES ON THEM THAT MARK WHERE OTHER TRUCKERS HAVE LOST THEIR LIVES.

THE LIFE OF AN ICE-ROAD TRUCKER MAY SEEM EXCITING AT FIRST, BUT MANY FIND IT TOO TOUGH AFTER A SEASON OR TWO OF LONG HOURS AND LITTLE SLEEP.

TURNOVER

Most ice-road truckers don't stay on the job for very long. It takes a special person with lots of knowledge about truck driving and cold weather to do the job well. For some, staying safe driving on regular roads is enough of a challenge!

TRAGEDY STRIKES

Accidents are never far from the thoughts of those who work on ice roads. In 2012, a British army gunner named Brett Colley was driving on an ice road when his truck went off the path, killing him.

Colley had watched *Ice-Road Truckers*, a show on the History Channel that follows the lives of ice-road drivers. He went to work in Alberta, Canada, hauling supplies on the ice roads. He was carrying food supplies when his truck drove off the road and continued down an **embankment**. A driver who was with Colley somehow managed to survive the crash.

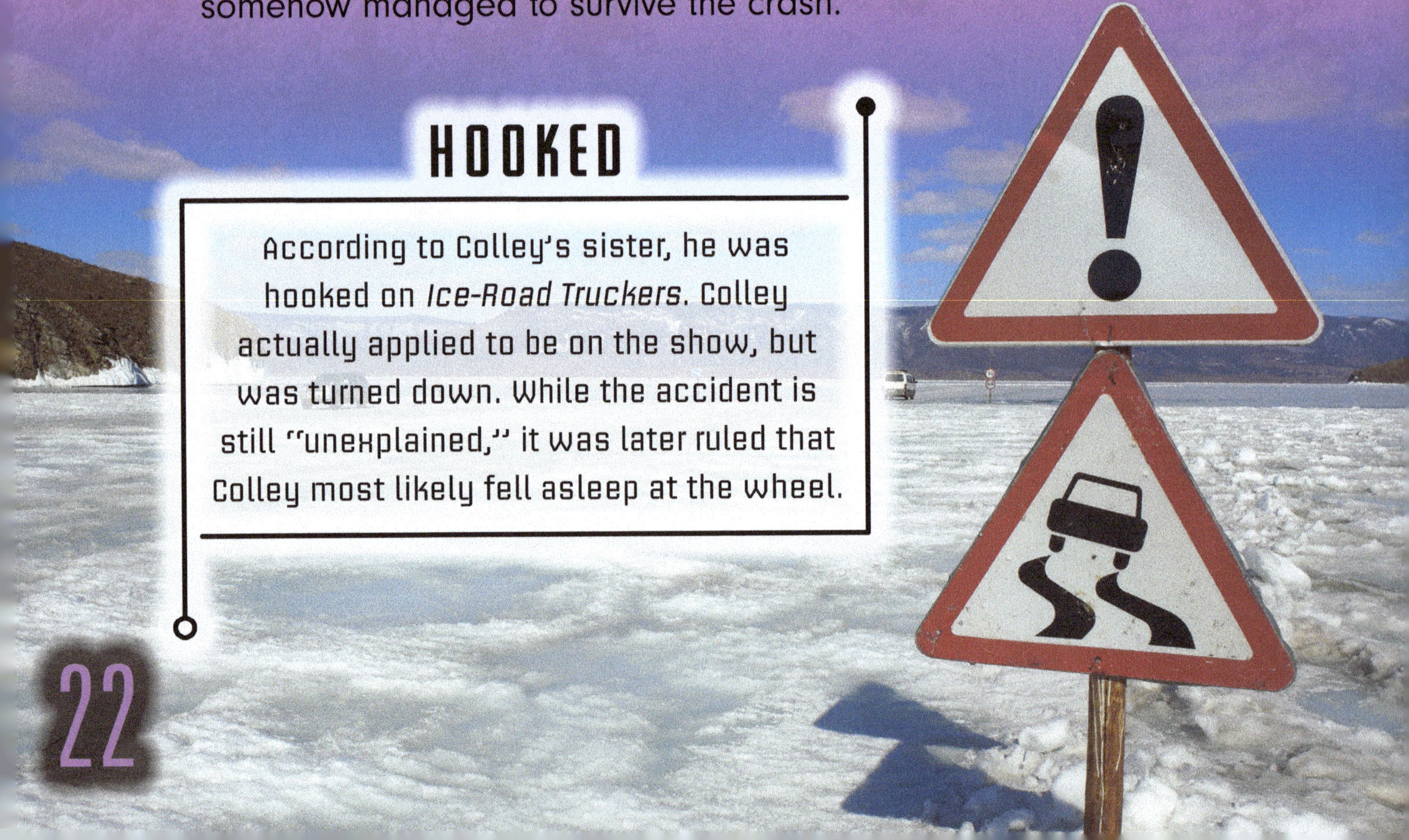

HOOKED

According to Colley's sister, he was hooked on *Ice-Road Truckers*. Colley actually applied to be on the show, but was turned down. While the accident is still "unexplained," it was later ruled that Colley most likely fell asleep at the wheel.

WHAT YOU MIGHT SEE ON TV AS NORMAL IS OFTEN A VERY DANGEROUS JOB. IT MIGHT BE FUN TO WATCH, BUT IT'S OFTEN MUCH HARDER TO DO IN REAL LIFE.

CLIMATE CHANGE

Climate change could have a serious effect on the ice roads. As recently as 2015, some ice roads in northern Canada were built several weeks late due to warm weather. While the weather could have been just an odd winter, climate scientists view it as a sign of things to come.

Ice-road crews are working on ways to adapt to the warming weather. Flooding the roads with more water to hasten the freezing process is a possibility, but it takes more work and costs more. Other options include a "fast lane" for trucks returning from dropping off a load and better monitoring of the thickness of the roads.

MELTING ICE ROAD IN CANADA

CLIMATE CHANGE MAY FURTHER SHORTEN THE ICE-ROAD SEASON IN THE FUTURE, LEADING TO MORE PROBLEMS FOR ICE-ROAD TRUCKERS.

OTHER OPTIONS

Climate change also has mining companies looking for new ways to bring in supplies if ice roads can't be built. Hovercraft, or cars that float above water or land, have been discussed, as well as floating aircraft called blimps. Scientists think areas able to hold ice roads will shrink as much as 13 percent by the middle of the 21st century.

HOVERCRAFT IN RUSSIA

ICE-ROAD TECHNOLOGY

Many people carry smartphones with them these days, and some scientists think this **technology** can help people driving on and building ice roads. Developed by the University of Alaska Fairbanks, an application, or app, lets oil companies and people who build ice roads know when it's safe to drive on ice in certain areas.

The app uses monitoring stations in Alaska and pairs information on soil temperatures, snow temperatures, and snow **density** to give people updates about ice-road conditions. The app shows this on a map and is used to decide when an ice surface is ready for road construction.

PROTECTED TUNDRA

The app was also made to protect areas where the ice roads run in Alaska. While ice roads may pass over lakes and rivers, they also run over marsh areas. The app allows users to see when travel on the roads will do the least harm to the **tundra** areas and animals nearby.

NOT ALL ICE ROADS ARE JUST FOR TRUCKS. FOR SOME PEOPLE LIVING IN DETTAH, A FISHING VILLAGE IN NORTHWESTERN CANADA, IT'S THE ONLY WAY TO GET HOME IN THE LONG WINTER MONTHS!

GOOD OR BAD?

Environmentalists, or those who want to protect nature, aren't big fans of ice roads. They point to fuel spills, wastewater, and air pollution as problems these roads bring to places few people have been. Others point to the effect of bringing people and machines into these places. It's unknown what the exact effect of ice roads is on the environment, but places like Alaska have taken steps to protect their tundra.

What do you think? Are the risks worth the reward with ice-road trucking? Protecting Earth is always important, but so are people's jobs. Which side do you fall on?

SOUTH POLE

An ice road from the United States' McMurdo Station to the South Pole was debated when the road was first planned a decade ago. Environmental groups worried about human waste and fuel spills, among other things, and asked for further studies. However, the road moved forward and is now in use.

ICE ROADS IN NORTH AMERICA

GLOSSARY

blowout: a large opening in ice caused by pressure from ice-road trucking

climate change: a gradual warming of Earth's atmosphere and oceans due in part to human activity

density: the amount of matter in a given area

embankment: a raised bank or wall built to carry a roadway

equipment: tools, clothing, and other items needed for a job

expert: someone with great knowledge about a certain subject

flexible: having the ability to bend easily

insulating: serving to prevent the exchange of heat

lattice: a structure made by crossing thin strips of wood or metal

monitor: to observe or check the quality

precaution: care taken in advance to prevent a problem

technology: tools used in the science of solving problems

tundra: cold, snowy northern lands that lack forests

FOR MORE INFORMATION

BOOKS

Gordon, Nick. *Ice Road Trucker*. Minneapolis, MN. Bellwether Media, Inc., 2013.

Ingram, Kevin. *Trucks*. Mankato, MN: Smart Apple Media, 2016.

WEBSITES

Ice Road Truck Jobs FAQ
iceroadtruckjobs.com/faq.htm
Think you'd like to drive a truck over an ice road? Read more about what it takes here.

Why Don't the Ice Road Truckers Just Fly?
history.co.uk/shows/ice-road-truckers/articles/why-dont-the-ice-road-truckers-just-fly
Find out more about ice-road truckers and how they work here.

Publisher's note to educators and parents: Our editors have carefully reviewed these websites to ensure that they are suitable for students. Many websites change frequently, however, and we cannot guarantee that a site's future contents will continue to meet our high standards of quality and educational value. Be advised that students should be closely supervised whenever they access the Internet.

INDEX